North American Wildlife Patterns for the Scroll Saw

by Lora S. Irish

Cover and gallery artwork by D. Thomson Penman.

ISBN 978-1-56523-165-8

Publisher's Cataloging-in-Publication Data

Irish, Lora S.

North American wildlife patterns for the scroll saw / by Lora S. Irish. --- 1st ed. -- EastPetersburg, PA : Fox Chapel Publishing, c2002.

p. ; cm.

ISBN: 978-1-56523-165-8 ; ISBN-10:1-56523-165-1

1. Wildlife wood-carving--Patterns. 2. Woodwork--Patterns. 3. Jig saws. 4. Wildlife art. 5. Animals in art. I. Title.

TT199.7 .I75 2002 2001097815
745.513--dc22 2008

To learn more about the other great books from Fox Chapel Publishing, or to find a retailer near you, call toll-free 800-457-9112 or visit us at *www.FoxChapelPublishing.com*.

We are always looking for talented authors. To submit an idea, please send a brief inquiry to acquisitions@foxchapelpublishing.com.

Printed in China
Eleventh printing

Table of Contents

About the Author

Lora S. Irish expresses her creativity in a number of mediums, including fabric, paint and wood. She worked for a number of years as a seminar instructor for an East Coast crafts distributor and later as a design director for a national needle art company. She has also published 13 limited edition fine art prints copyrighted through the Library of Congress.

Currently Lora is a free-lance artist under her own company name, Art Designs Studio. She focuses on creating original oil canvases, acrylic paintings and sign crafting. She and her husband, Mike, established **www.carvingpatterns.com**, a pattern website for carvers and other woodworkers. All of the patterns and artwork featured here are originals designed by Lora.

Lora has also published several other books for scrollers, including *The Great Book of Dragon Patterns* and *World Wildlife Patterns for the Scroll Saw*. Her pattern and how-to books for carvers include *Landscapes in Relief*, *Wildlife Carving in Relief*, *Classic Carving Patterns*, *Chip Carving Classics One* and *Chip Carving Classics Two*.

Introduction

With just a little wood, a pattern, and a scroll saw any woodworker can bring the wonderful animals that share our world to life on boxes, corner brackets, and wall decor. The simple silhouette style of the scroll saw pattern is excellent for reflecting the flowing lines of muscles and fur.

Feathers can be delineated to give birds and eagles flight. Ears can be tilted forward or laid back to give wolves and deer expression. Full scenes with habitat areas, the animals and a background of mountains and sky all can be created from one continuous piece of wood.

North America offers a wide variety of animal life to use in our art form. Pesky raccoons can hide in the hollow of the old tree and the graceful elongated stalk of the mountain lion can be captured against the rocky ledge. Somewhere within the pages of this pattern book you will find your favorite North American animal. Those animals and birds that are so very popular in today's art—such as the whitetail deer, the black bear, the pheasant and many others—can be found in several different patterns to provide a wide choice of ideas.

These patterns are created so that they can be easily used individually or added to corner brackets, weathervane arrows and framed edges. Use your imagination as you browse through the pages for the numerous adaptations that you can add to make each work a unique piece of art. Most of all please have some fun as you use these designs.

If you're looking for help with the basics of scrolling, I highly recommend the following publications: *Scroll Saw Woodworking & Crafts* magazine (formerly *Scroll Saw Workshop*) or *Scroll Saw Workbook* by John A. Nelson, both published by Fox Chapel Publishing, 1-800-457-9112, **www.FoxChapelPublishing.com**.

– Lora S. Irish

Smokey

(Black Bear)

Warning Signs

(Grizzly Bear)

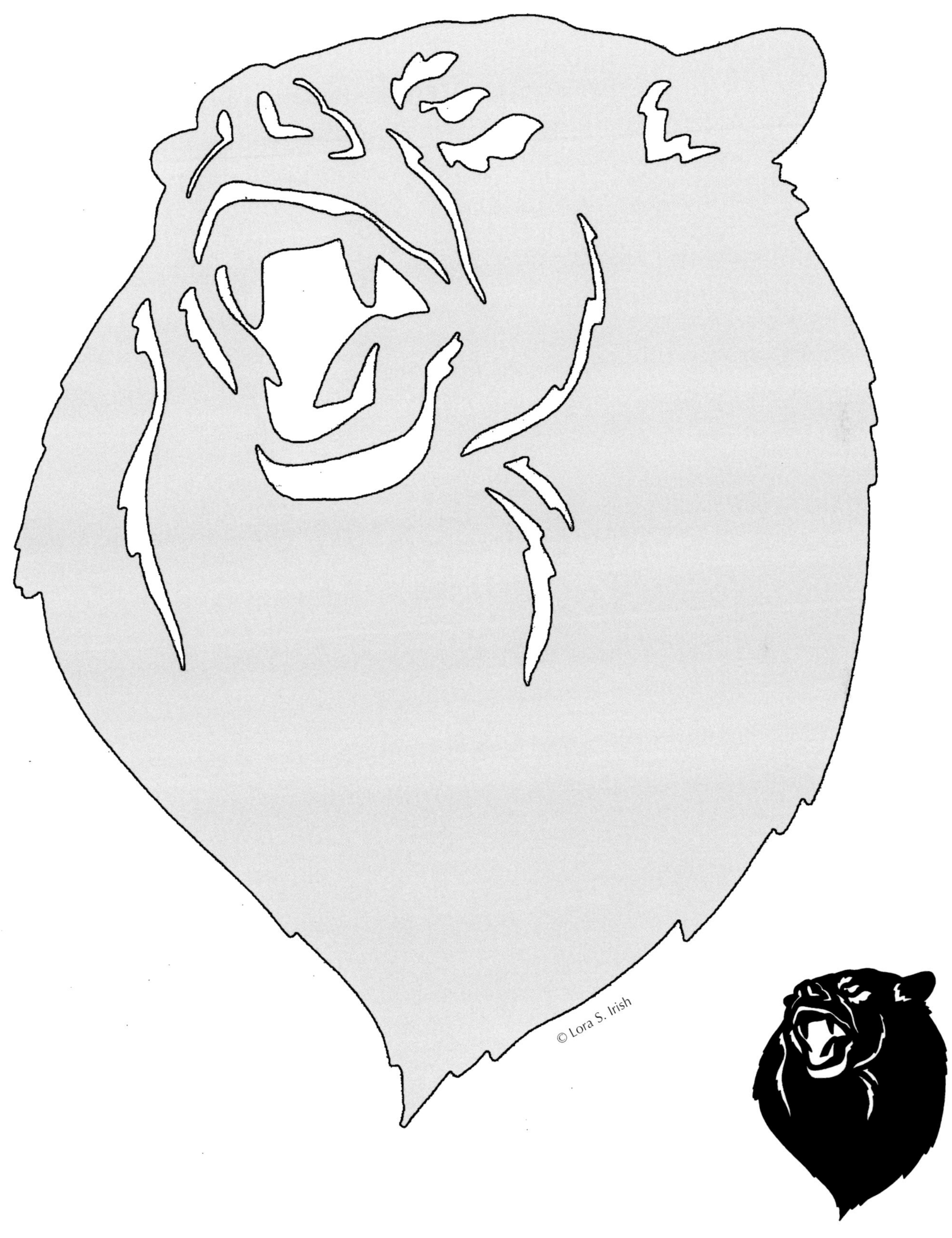

The Long Walk

(Black Bear)

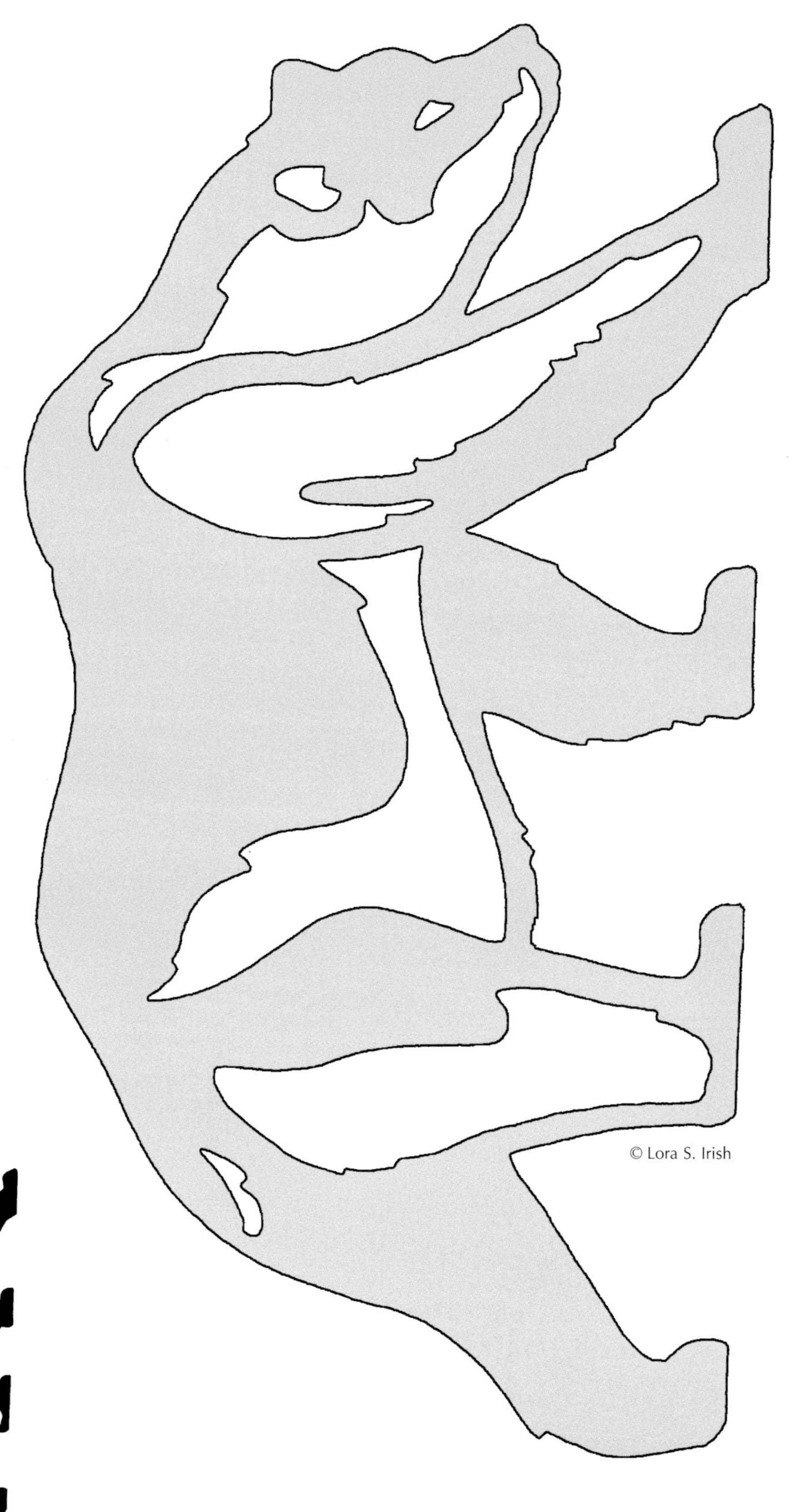

Evergreen Trail

(Grizzly Bear)

Timber...

(Beaver)

© Lora S. Irish

King of the Mountain

(Bobcat)

© Lora S. Irish

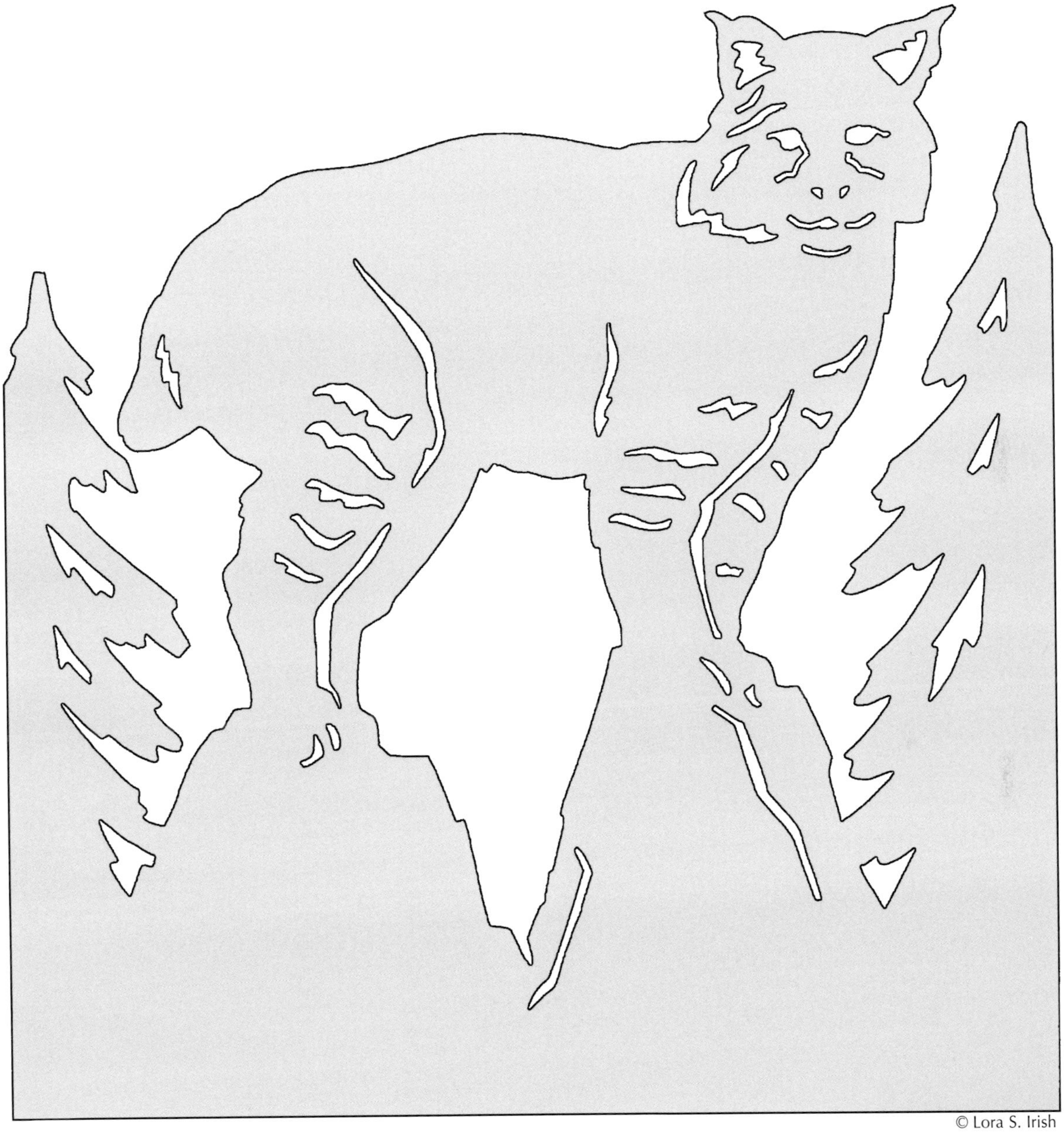

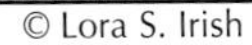

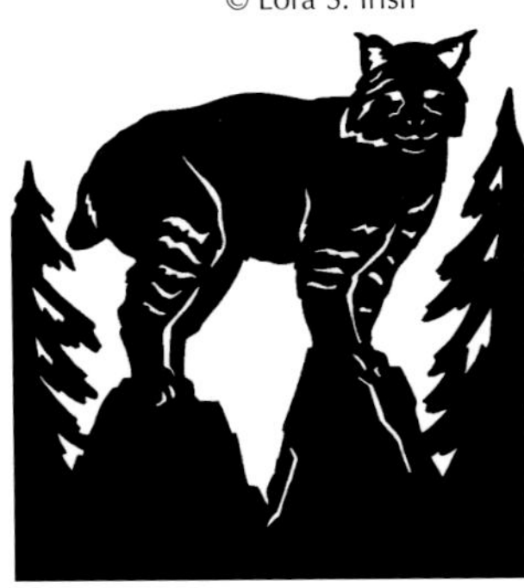

Up a Tree

(Bobcat)

Prairie King

(Buffalo)

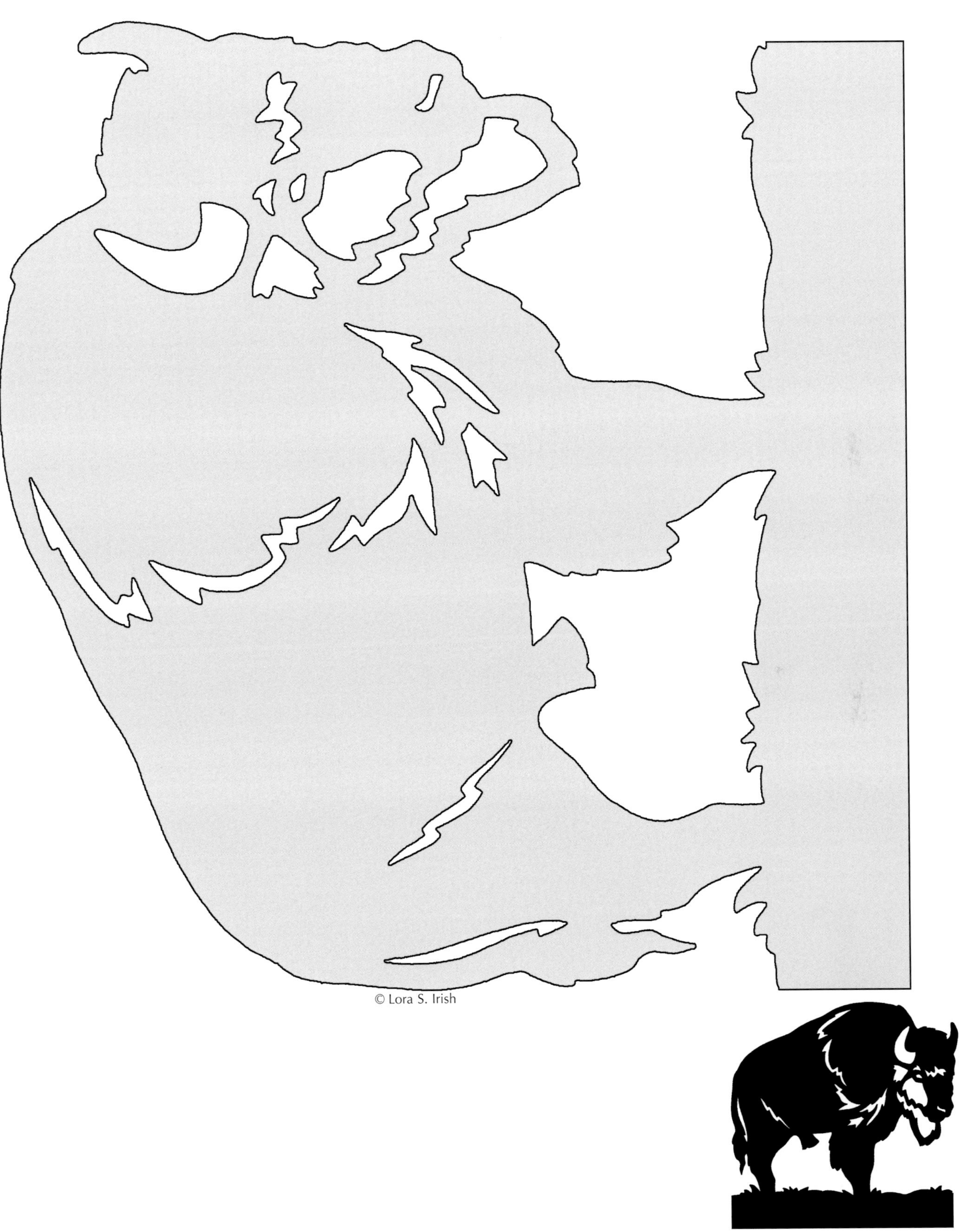

Still Waters

(Canada Goose)

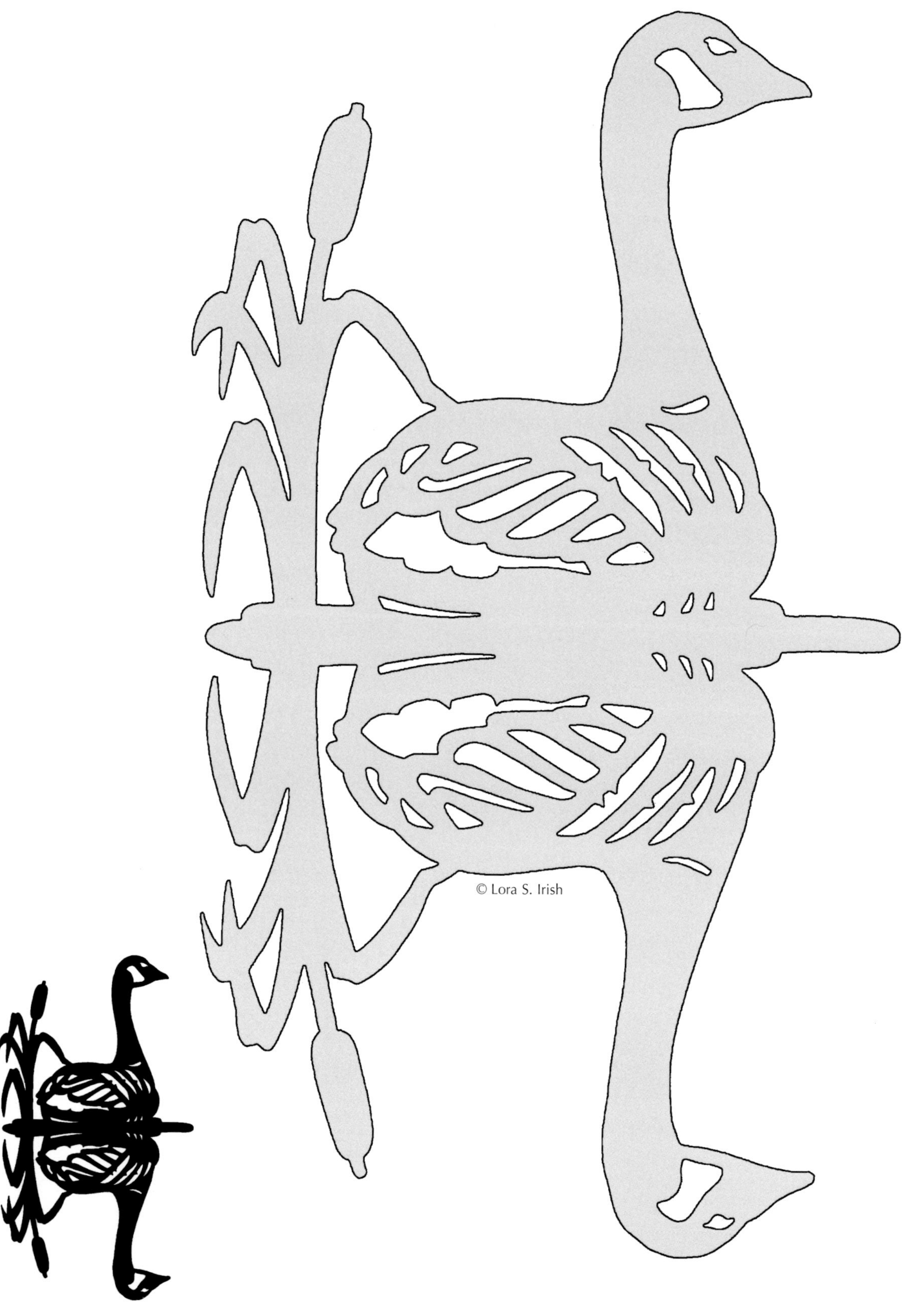

Autumn Flight

(Canada Goose)

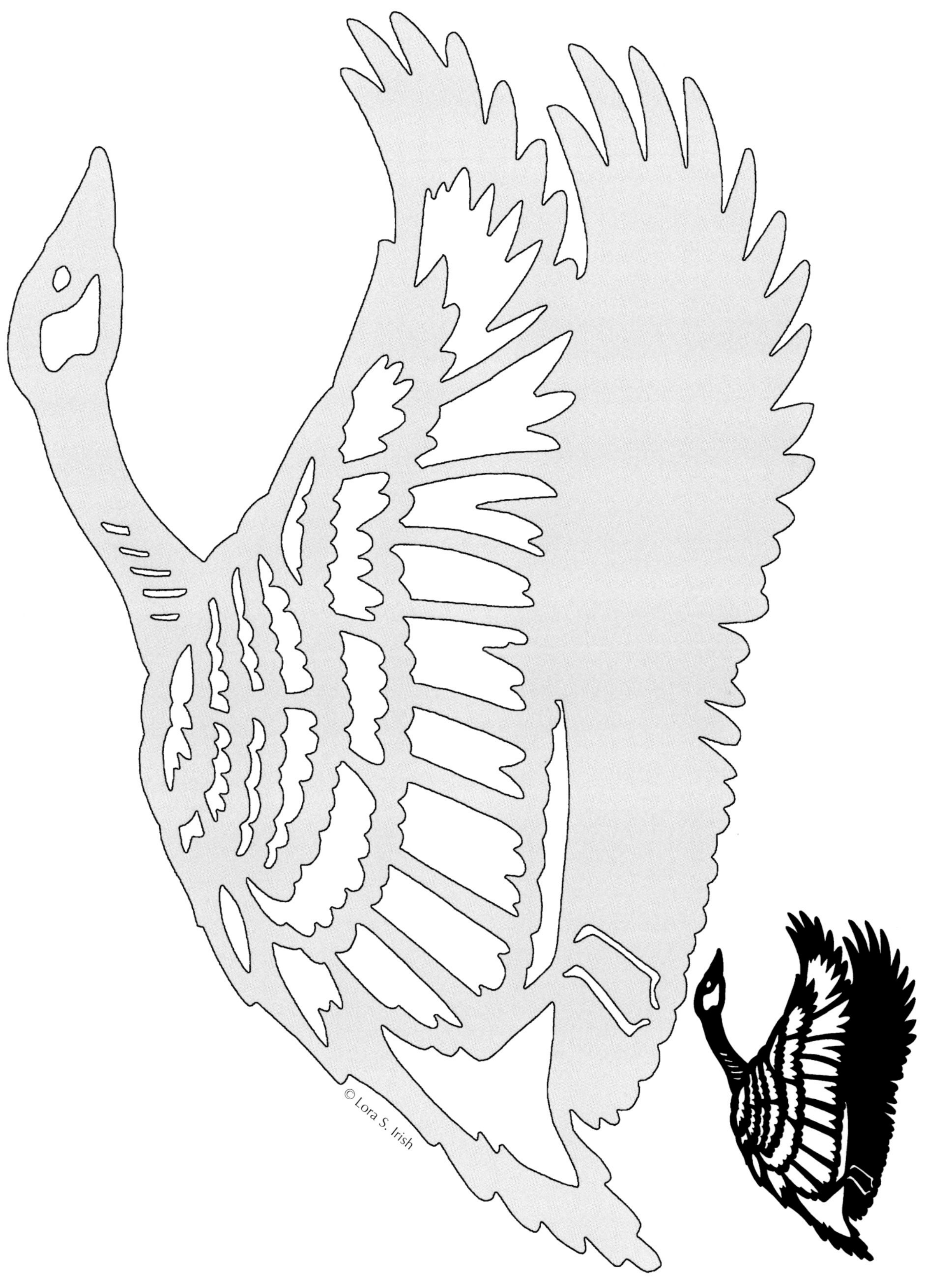

Bucking the System

(Whitetail Deer)

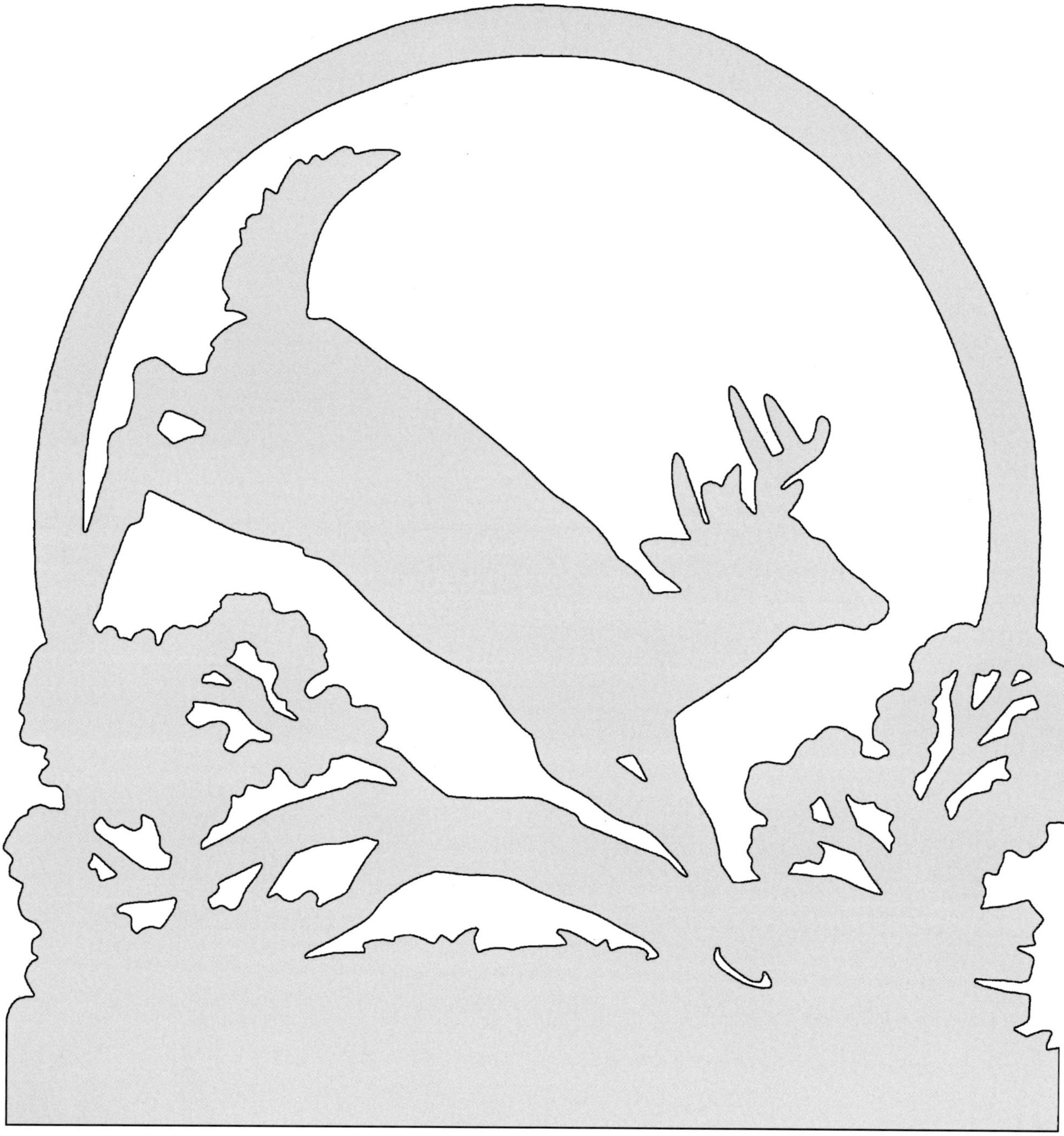

© Lora S. Irish

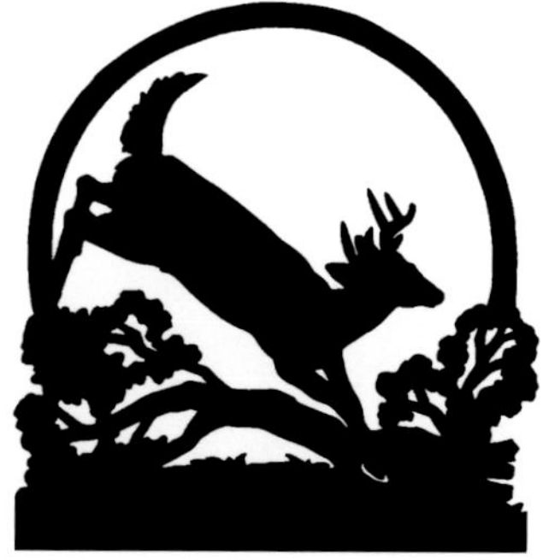

Stylized Buck

(Whitetail Deer)

Pine Tree Path

(Whitetail Deer)

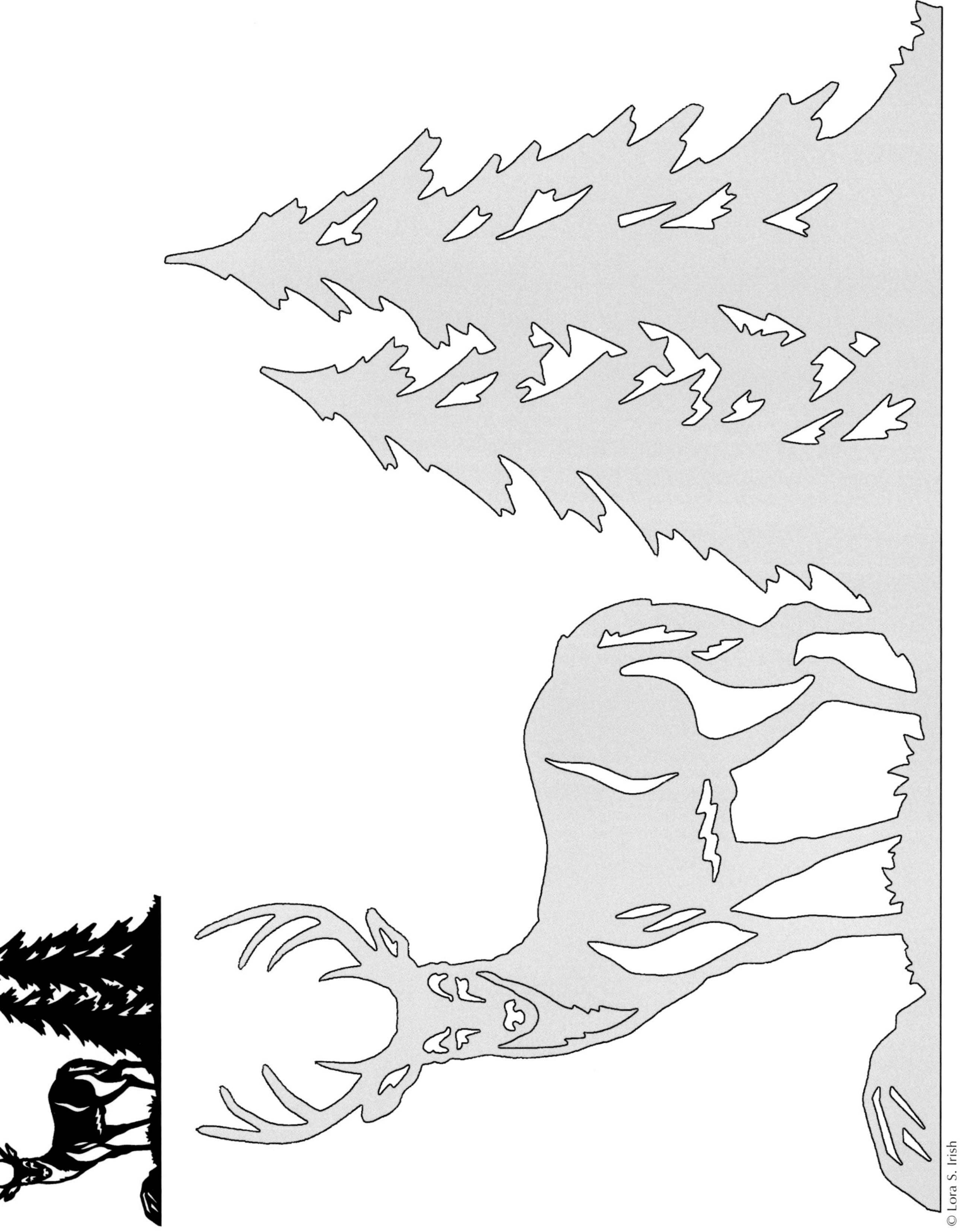

Ready for Splash Down

(Mallard Duck)

Flying High

(Mallard Duck)

Nesting Teal

(Greenwing Teal Duck)

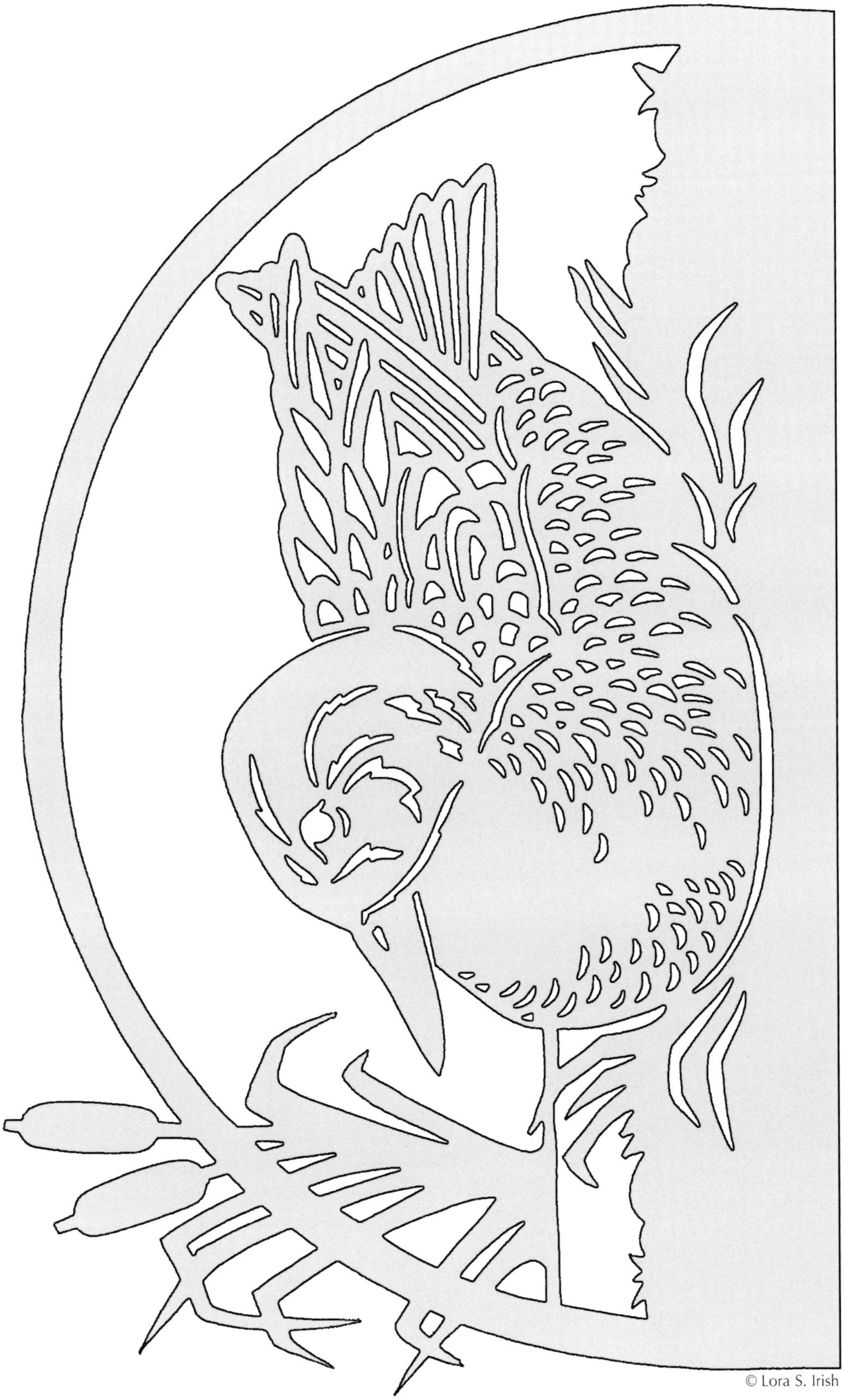

© Lora S. Irish

Redhead Roost

(Redhead Duck)

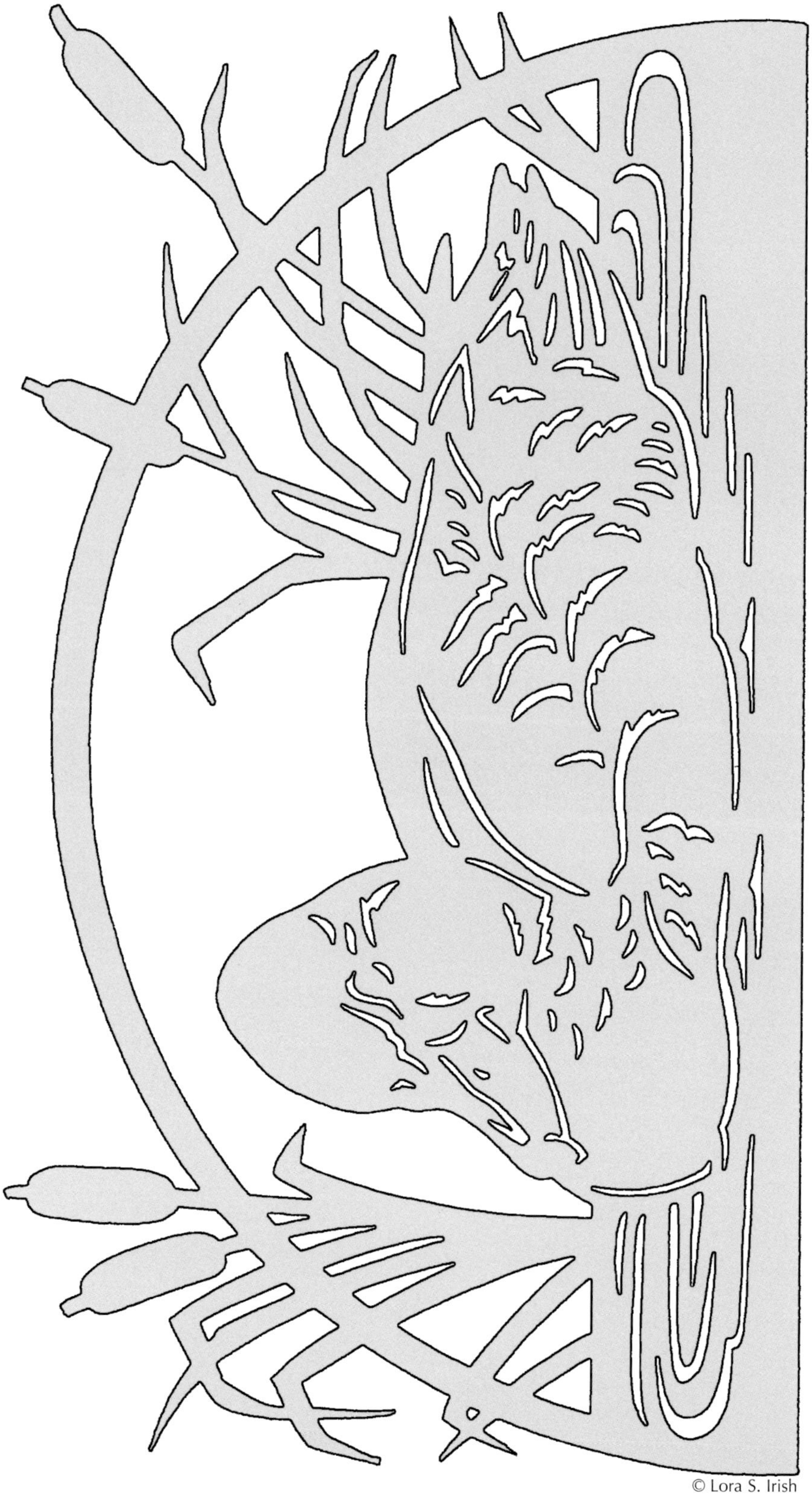

© Lora S. Irish

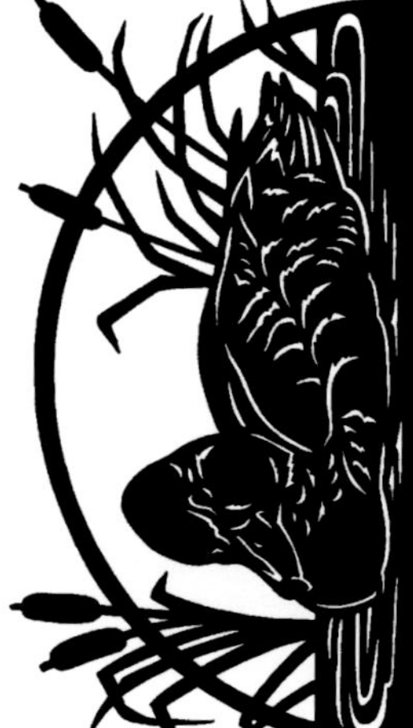

Stylized Drake

(Pintail Duck)

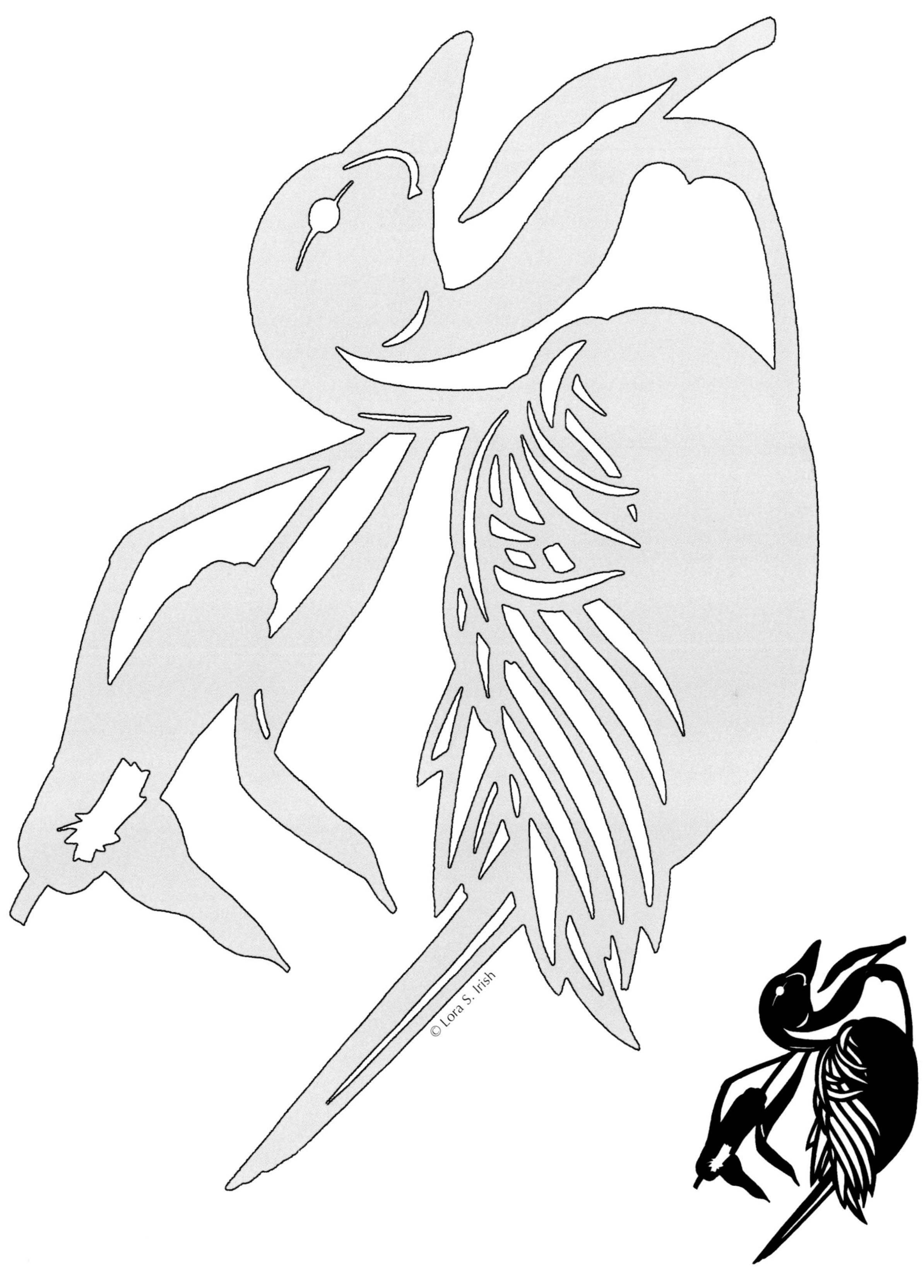

Rising Star

(Wood Duck)

© Lora S. Irish

Mean and Lean

(American Bald Eagle)

Florida Flash

(Flamingo)

On the Prowl

(Red Fox)

Gentle Ripples

(Goose)

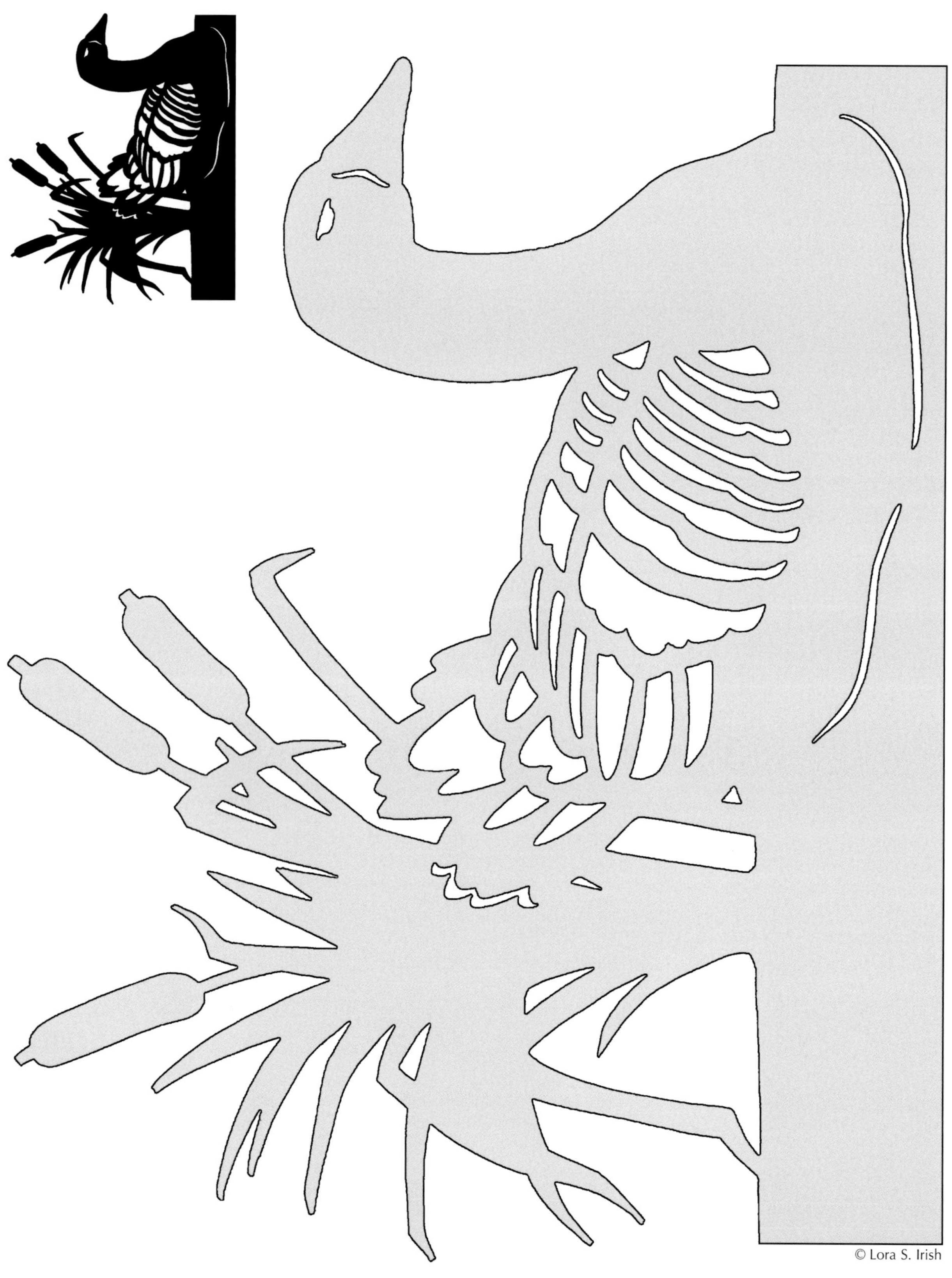

Blue Plumes

(Blue Heron)

Blazed Portrait

(Mustang Horse)

Derby Sprint

(Horse)

Glacier Lake

(Bull Moose)

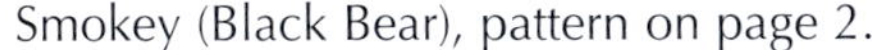

Smokey (Black Bear), pattern on page 2.

Gold and White Royalty (Pronghorn), pattern on page 46.

Redhead Roost (Redhead Duck), pattern on page 18.

Prairie King (Buffalo), pattern on page 9.

Blazed Portrait (Mustang Horse), pattern on page 26.

Stylized Drake (Pintail Duck) cut as a corner bracket, pattern on page 19.

Moonlight Stalk (Mountain Lion), pattern on page 47.

High Mountain Monarch (Mountain Lion), pattern on page 48.

Pine Tree Path (Whitetail Deer), pattern on page 14.

Snow Ghost (Timber Wolf), pattern on page 67.

Giving a Hoot (Owl), pattern on page 37.

Garden Patrol (Box Turtle), pattern on page 64.

Twists and Turns (Tern), pattern on page 61.

Mean and Lean (American Bald Eagle), pattern on page 21.

Northern Exposure

(Bull Moose)

Royal Crown

(Bull Moose)

Night Silhouette

(Owl)

Giving a Hoot

(Horned Owl)

Old Salty

(Pelican)

Texas Terror

(Eastern Rattlesnake)

Country Splendor

(Ring Neck Pheasant)

Rail to Rail

(Ring Neck Pheasant)

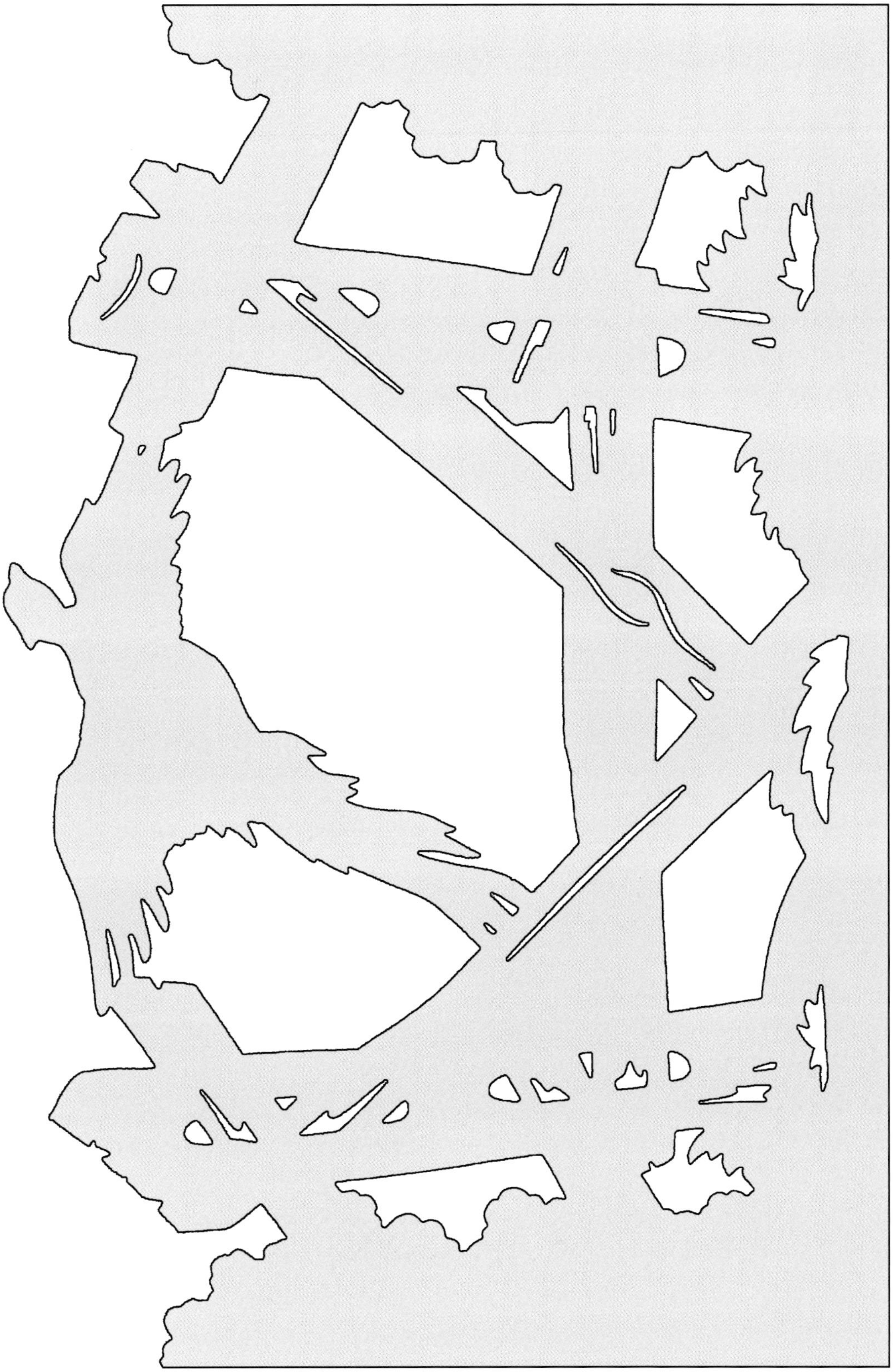

Corn Stalk Cover

(Ring Neck Pheasant)

© Lora S. Irish

Burst Into Flight

(Ring Neck Pheasant)

Puff and Stuff

(Prairie Chicken)

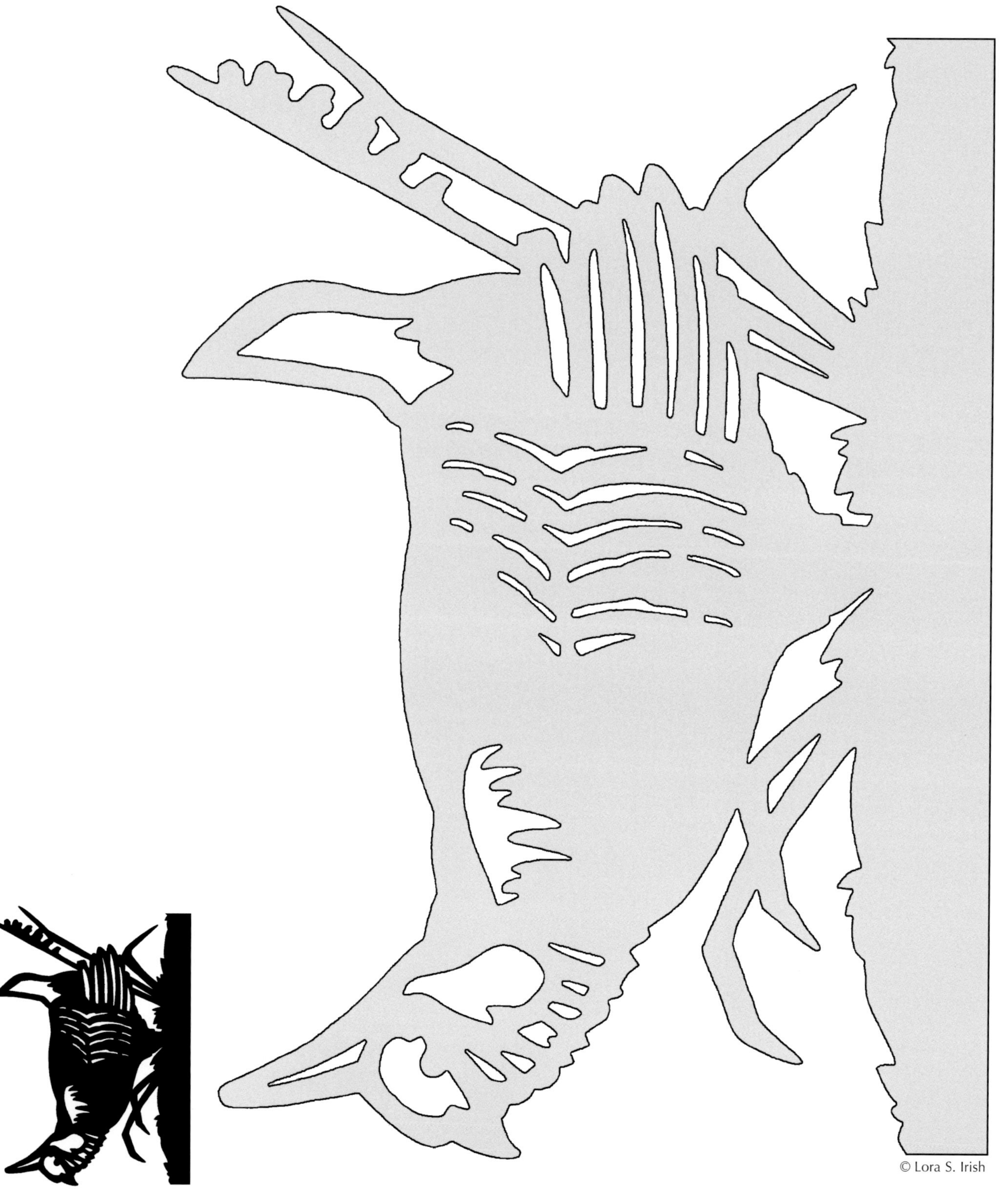

Outpost

(Prairie Dog)

Gold and White Royalty

(Pronghorn)

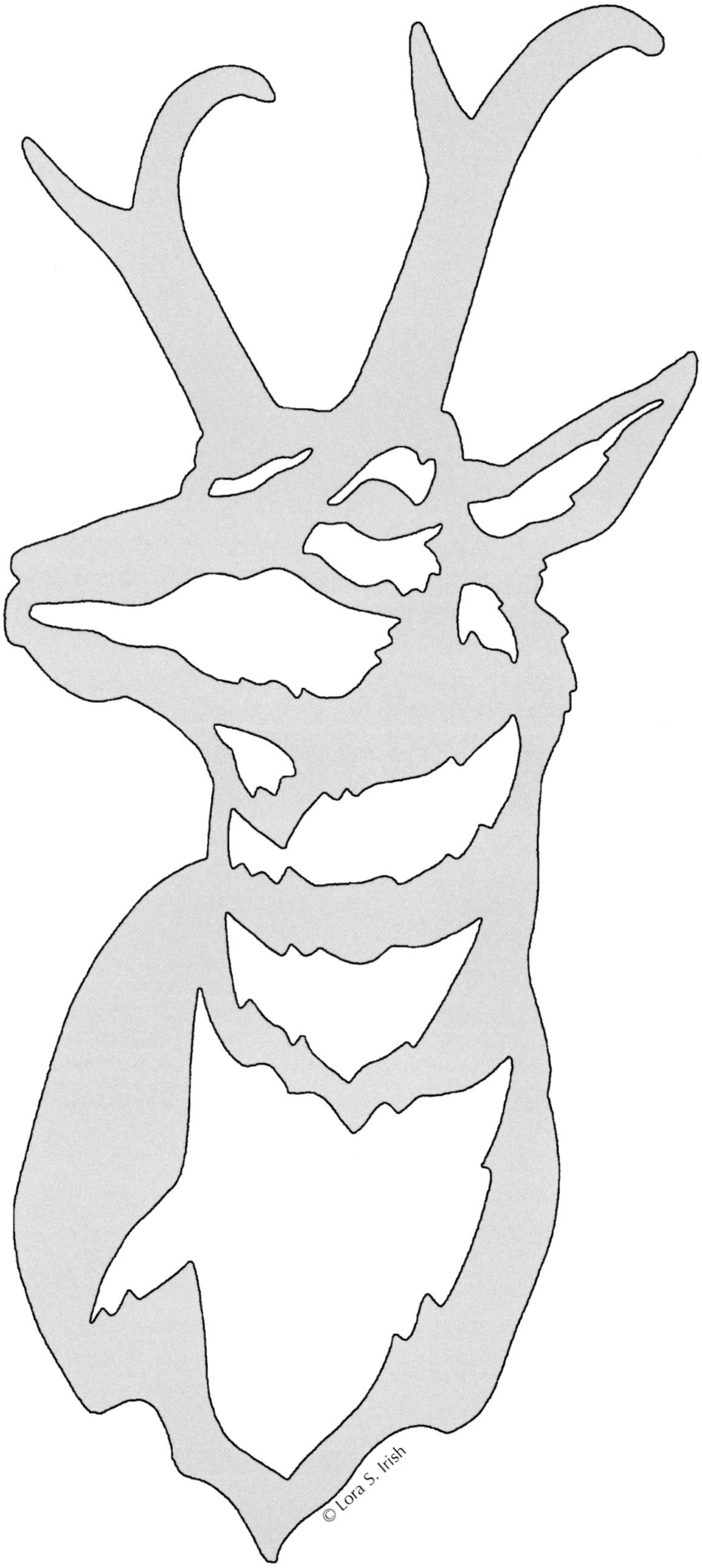

Moonlight Stalk

(Mountain Lion)

High Mountain Monarch

(Mountain Lion)

Up, Up and Away

(Bobwhite Quail)

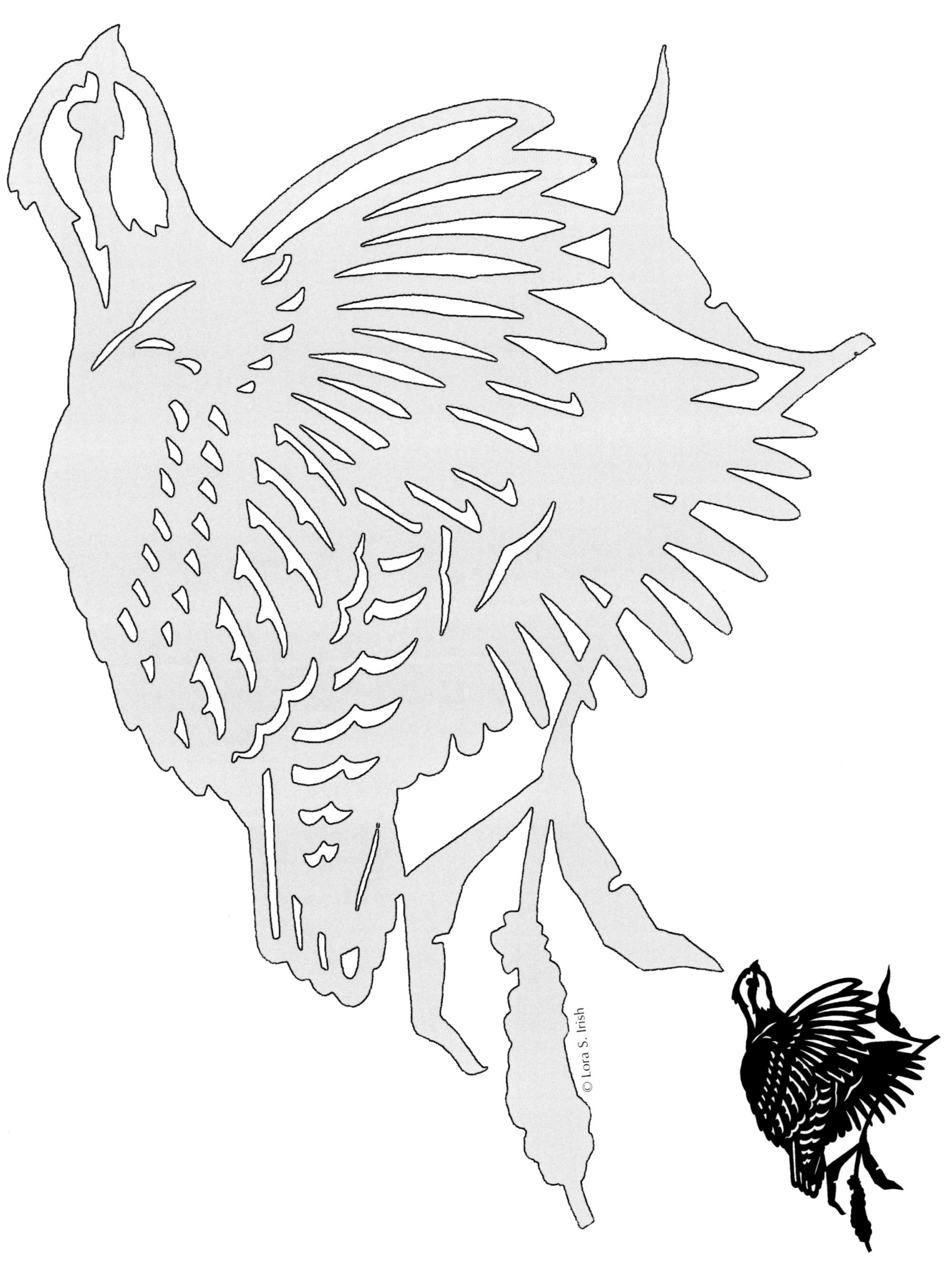

California Gold

(California Quail)

Cottontail Express

(Eastern Cottontail)

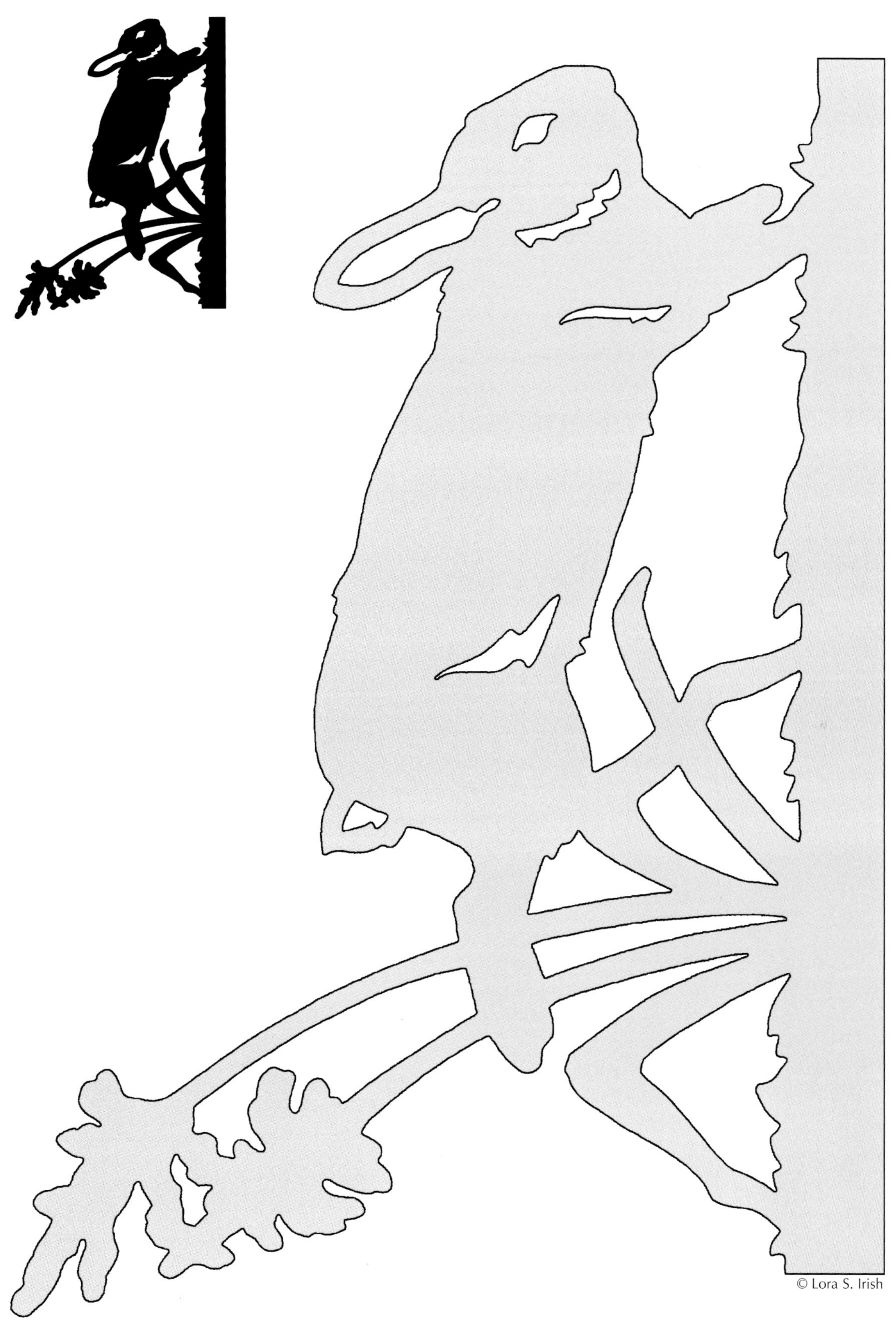

Rocky Refuge

(Big Horn Sheep)

Big Horn Portrait

(Big Horn Sheep)

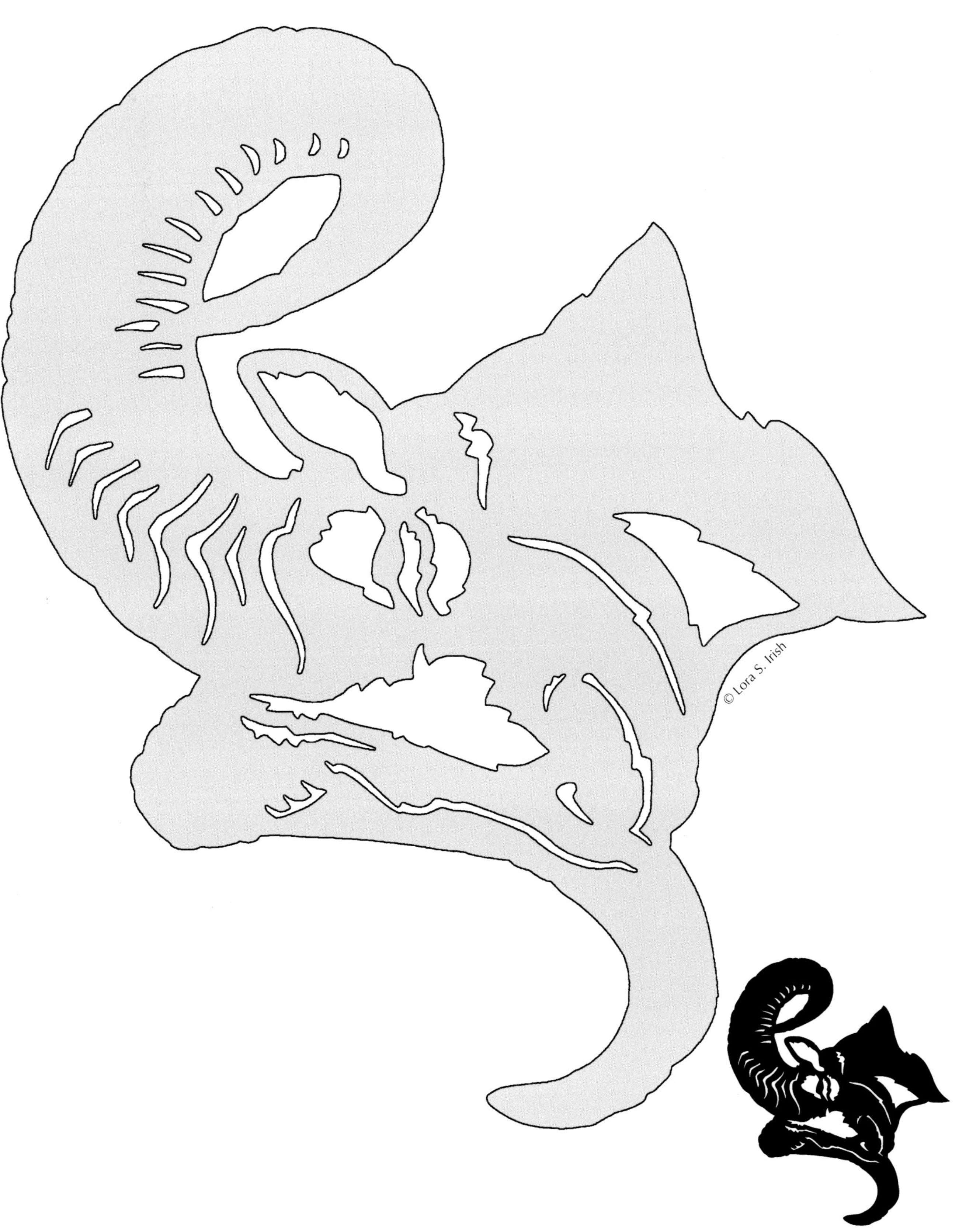

Narrow Ledge

(Mountain Goat)

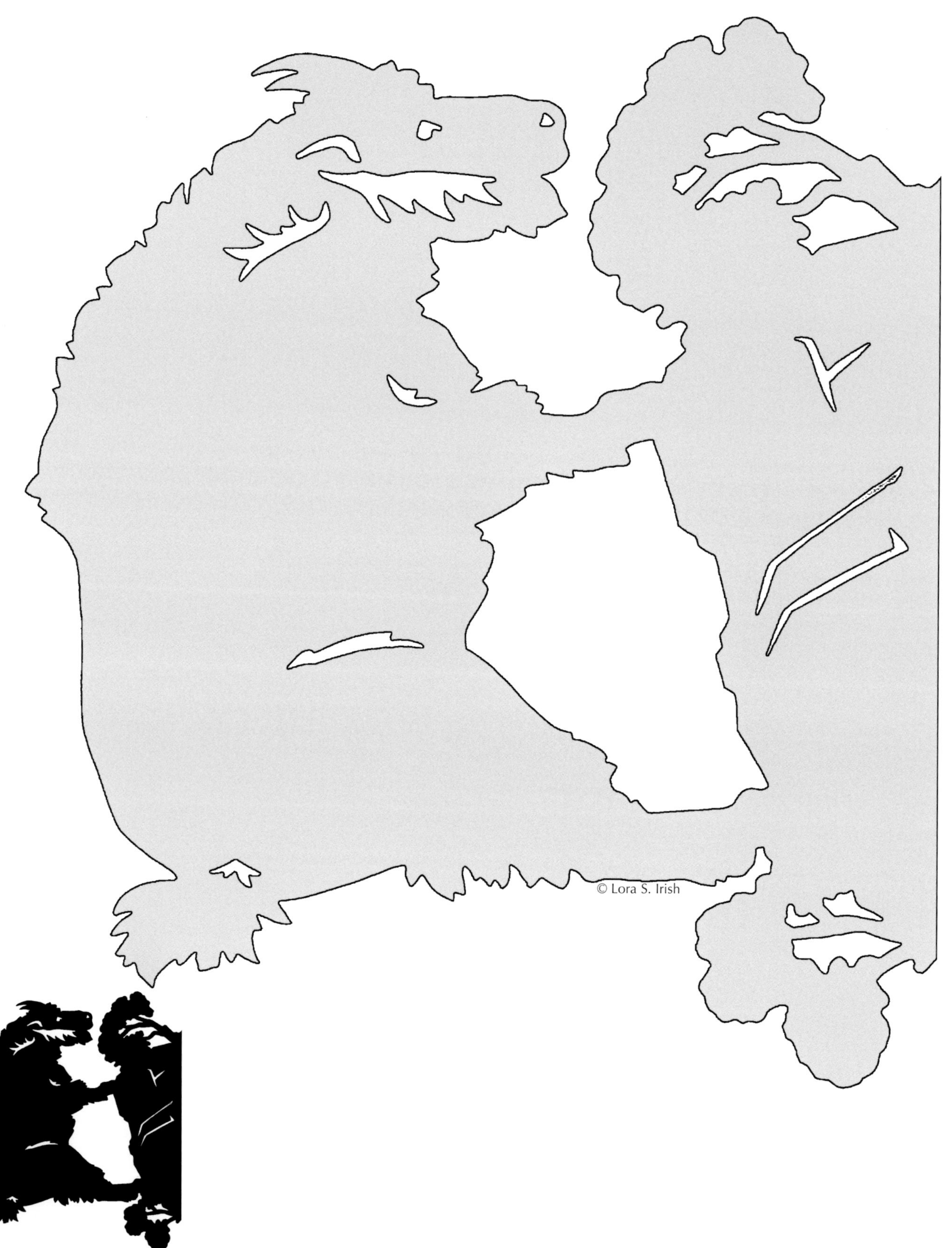

Dinner Preparations

(Raccoon)

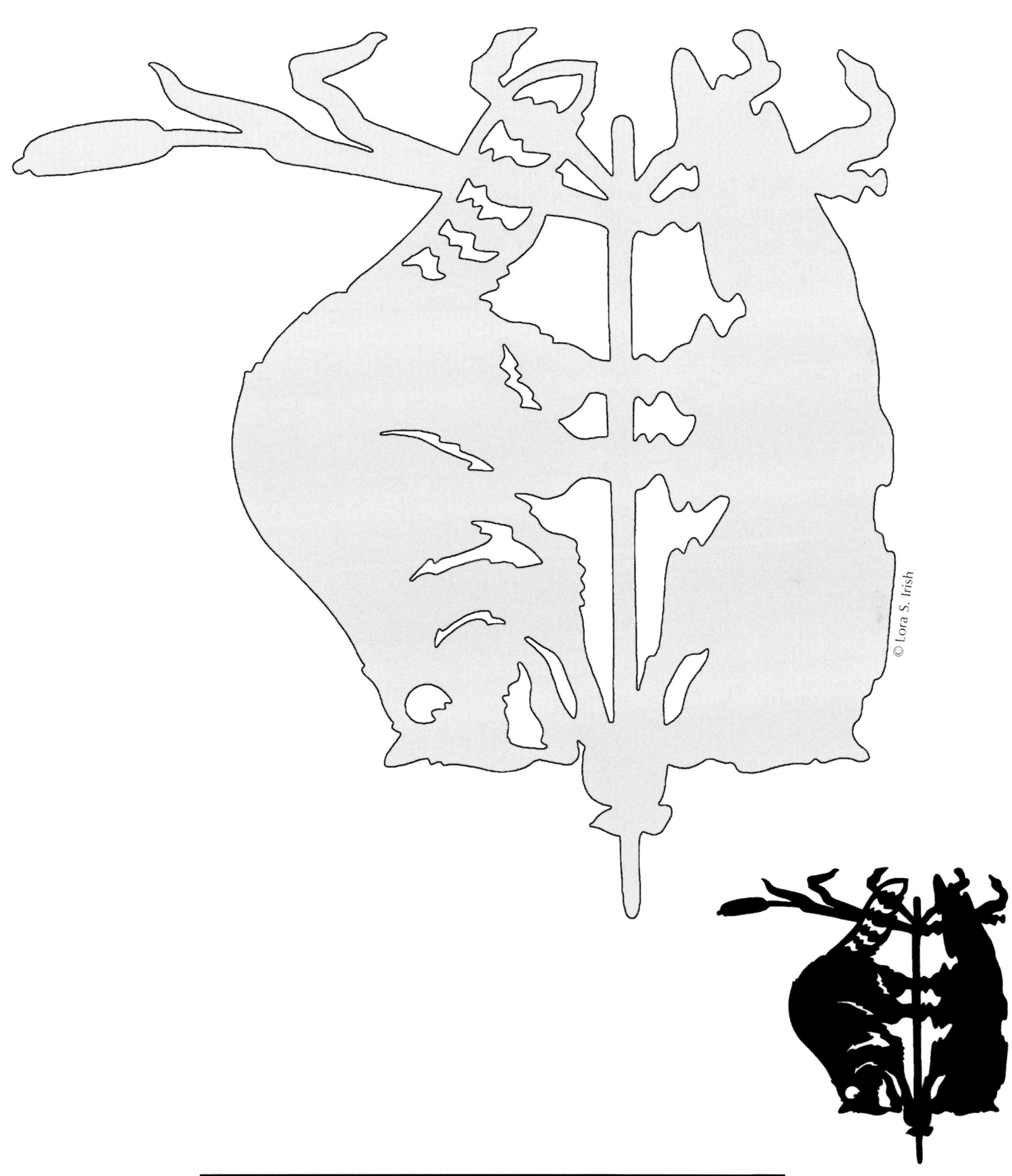

Peek-A-Boo

(Raccoon)

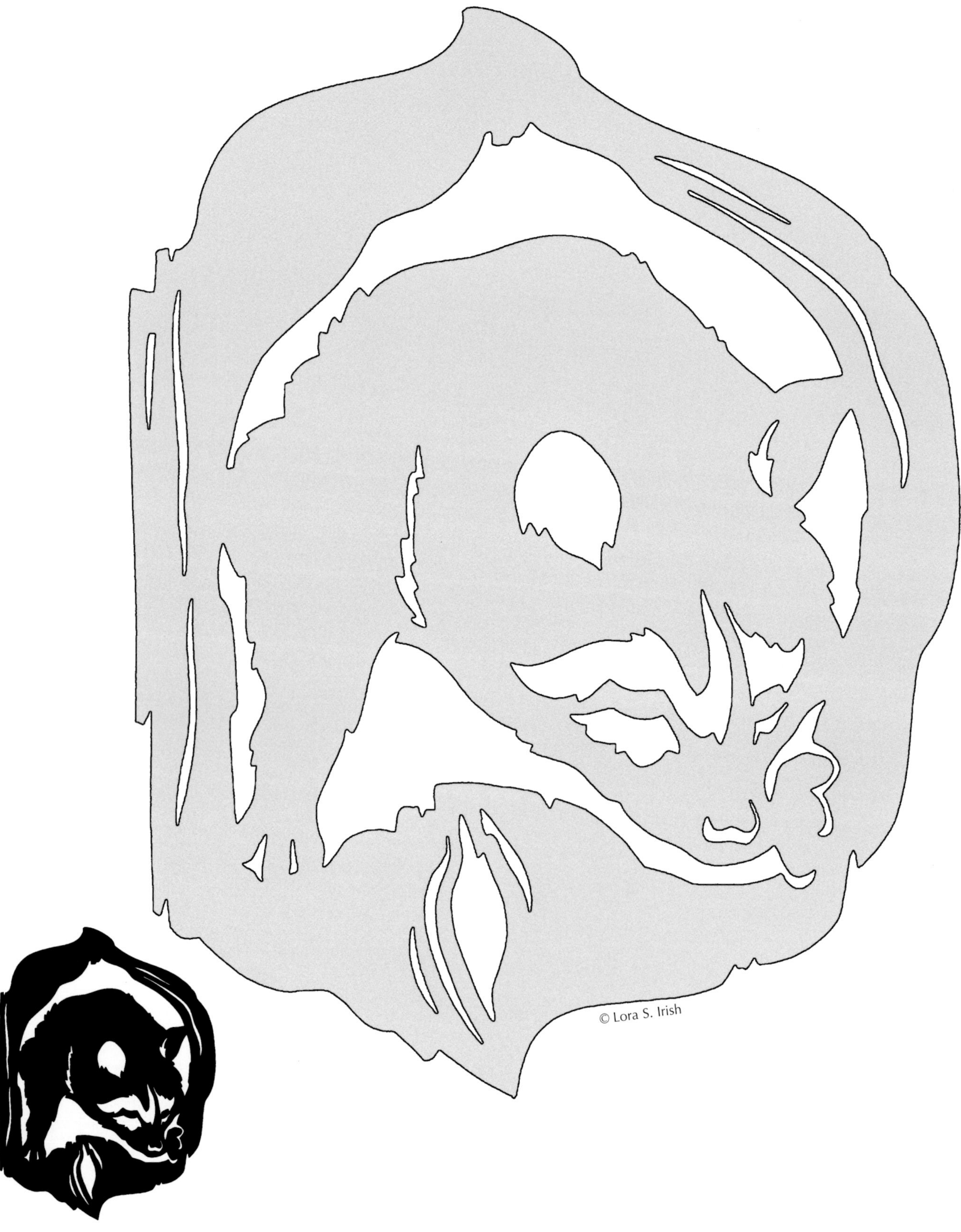

Toxic Fumes

(Skunk)

Saying Grace

(Gray Squirrel)

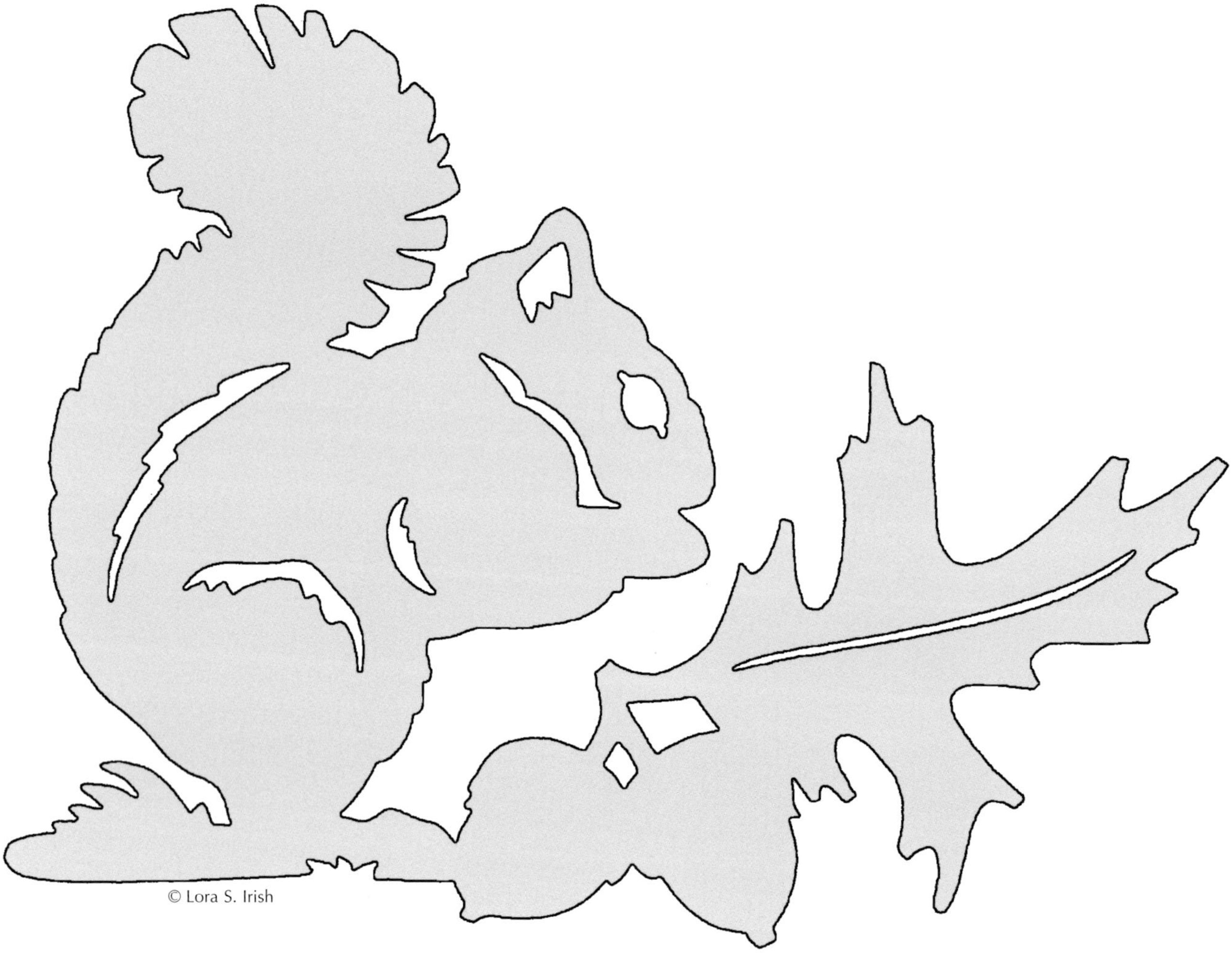

Balancing Act

(Gray Squirrel)

Reflections of the Heart

(Trumpeter Swan)

Twists and Turns

(Tern)

Ruffled Display

(Turkey)

© Lora S. Irish

Fence Line Flight

(Turkey)

Garden Patrol

(Box Turtle)

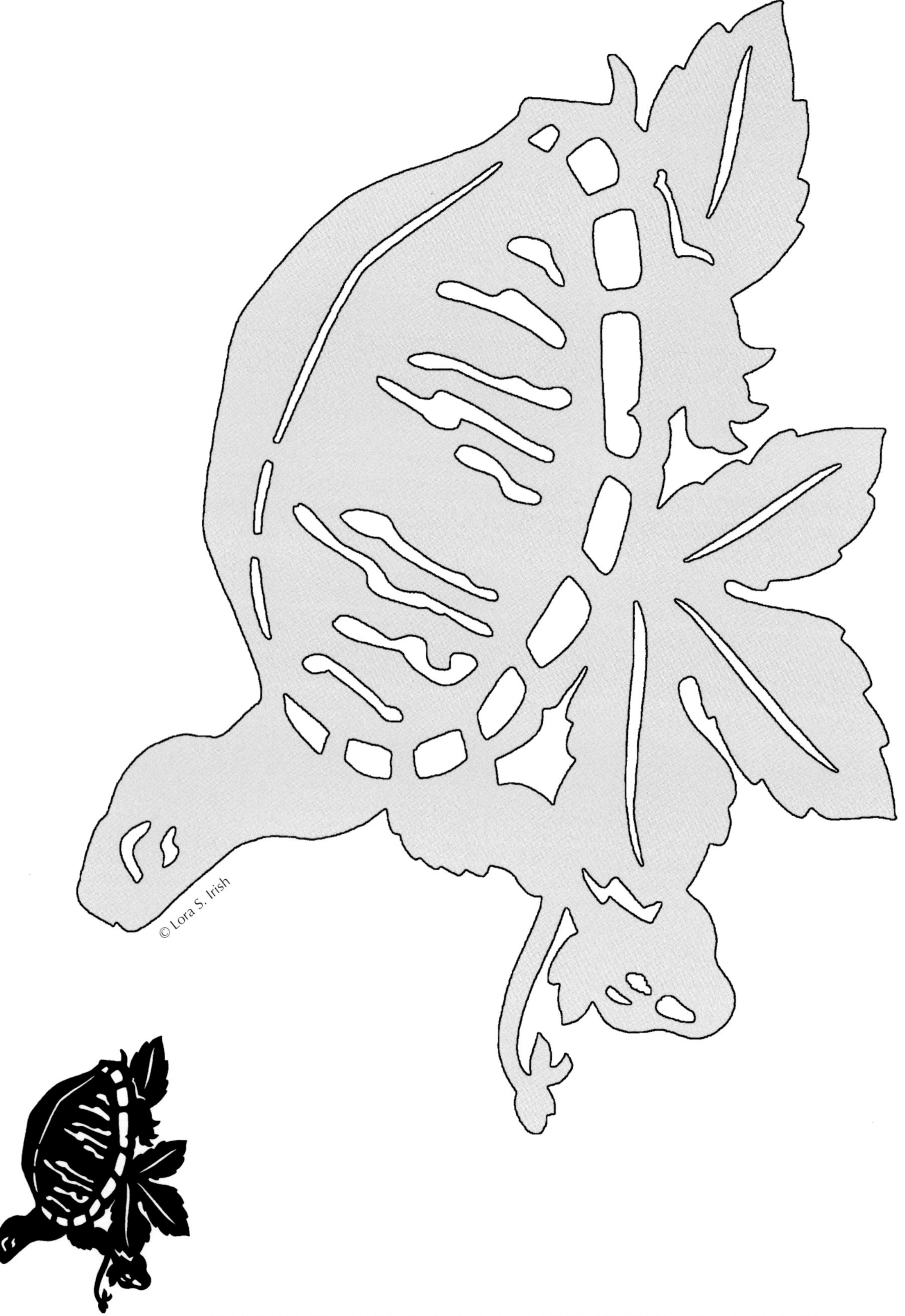

Howling at the Moon

(Timber Wolf)

Hidden Den

(Timber Wolf)

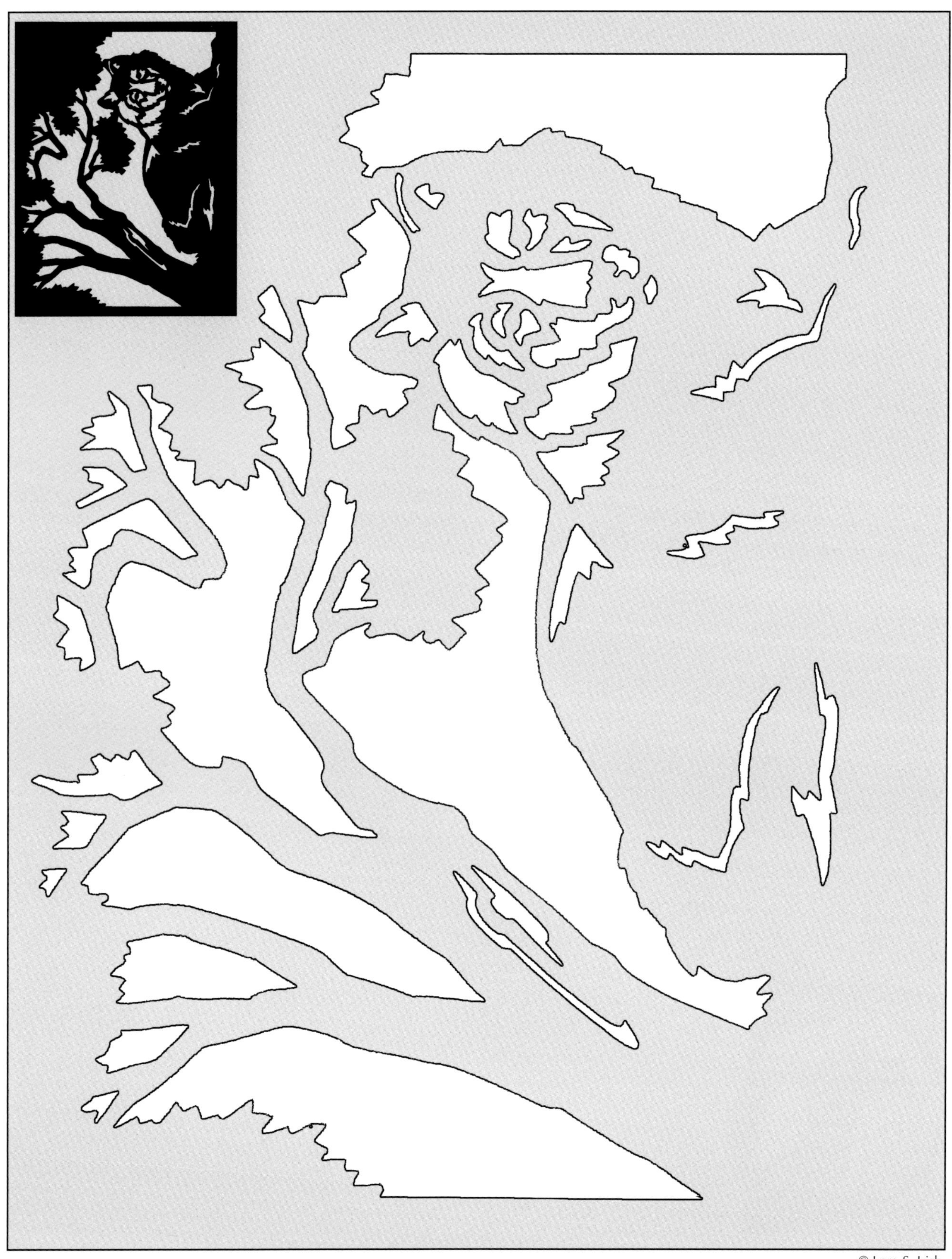

Snow Ghost

(Timber Wolf)